Emotional Intelligence for kids

RESILIENCE

Facing challenges

HELLO,

Welcome to the e-Learning Emotional Intelligence Program by KeyWords Education.

Our goal is to help parents, teachers and children realize that there are relationships between what they think, what they feel and the way they behave.

Those who know their own emotions and thoughts are better prepared to make good choices and to relate appropriately to others in an increasingly complex and dynamic world.

The purpose of KeyWords is to create a unique moment of mutual learning between parents and children about the Set of skills called socioemotional skills, which are increasingly important for life in society.

Neuroscience has proven that Socioemotional skills can be learned. This is an emotional skills program that will teach your child about socioemotional domains such as self-knowledge, self-control, empathy, determination, and resilience, helping him or her to make more responsible decisions and develop social skills.

THE BENEFITS

SELF-KNOWLEDGE
--- Increases confidence and self-esteem
--- Helps children to understand thei limitations and strengths
--- Increased perseverance and encouragement to take responsibility

SELF-CONTROL
--- Reduces impulsivity, generating attitudes more appropriate to the objectives
--- Decreased anxiety and improved self-esteem

RESPONSIBLE DECISION-MAKING
--- Prepares children to assess the consequences and make constructive choices
--- Increased focus and ability to make good choices

SOCIAL SKILLS
--- Contribute to healthy relationships, stimulating cooperation, Clear communication and the ability to withstand pressure
---Knowledge of how to deal with "NO" and the frustrations of life
--- Healthier, more accomplished and more successful people
--- Greater perception of family values in relation to school

EMPATHY
--- Teaches children to understand other people's points of view
--- Helps to createstrong links between people

LEARN MORE ABOUT THIS EBOOK

SECTIONS

LET'S START

In this section, the parent(s) and teacher(s) conduct a conversation with children to spark Interest in the issues that will be addressed.

UNDERSTANDING THE CONCEPT

Here, using simple language (and, whenever possible, with a playful tone), we introduce the main concepts that will be discussed with the children.

LET'S TALK

In this section, parent(s) and teacher(s) talk about the concept of this class with the children.

CONCLUSION

Here, we draw conclusions about the concept and provide activities on the subject of the class.

EPISODES

NAME THAT EMOTION Recognizing your emotions	**WORRY & ANXIETY** In search of emotional balance
MANAGING FEAR Overcoming this challenge	**SELF-REGULATION** Controlling impulses
MANAGING CONFLICT Seeking a positive solution	**ACCEPTANCE** Redefining your visions
RESILIENCE Facing challenges	**EMPATHY** If you were them…

KINDNESS A new way to see the world	**GRATITUDE** This is the secret to life
COOPERATION Building partnerships	**BEDTIME BATTLES**
HARD TIMES WITH HOMEWORK	**MEALTIME** Like or dislike?
FRUSTRATION Managing NO	**SIBLINGS** Handling jealousy

SECTION: LET'S START
RESILIENCE – FACING CHALLENGES

It would be great if we could have control of every situation we go through.
But this is impossible. There are things that happen and we cannot change them.
We must accept them and move on.

This ability to go through difficult times and "get through it" has a name: it's resilience. Resilient people are those who are able to overcome difficulties, learn from them and to adapt, finding alternative solutions to solve their problems.

Certainly, you will still fall a few times in your life. Sometimes the falls will be literal. The important thing is to understand that problems are part of everyone's life and that it is possible to learn from difficult situations.

This learning makes us better people.

SECTION: UNSTANDING THE CONCEPT

RESILIENCE

"Optimists and pessimists die in exactly the same way, but they live very different lives."

This thought by Shimon Peres, Nobel Peace Prize winner and former president of Israel, is related to elasticity or resilience.

In physics, the concept corresponds to the property that some materials have that allows them to bend without breaking and, later, return to their original form. In the case of people, resilience is the ability to face adverse situations that can push us to the limit, overcome them with balance and come out of them even stronger.

Resilience is an attitude that can be developed throughout life. We learn in practice every time we go through challenges and failures and decide to move on.
The first lessons in resilience must be given in childhood.

Let's think about your daily routine. Have you ever needed to be resilient? Have you ever experienced a difficult situation and learned something from it? You probably answered yes. We all have good and bad times. And inthe end, we learned from them.

Being resilient is more than being resistant. Be careful not to confuse the two words. Resistant people withstand pressure, "stay tight" and resist. Resilient ones go further: they are pressured, they adapt, they are flexible, they learn from difficulties and find solutions to move on.

WALT DISNEY

We will start our list with the founder of one of the greatest entertainment empires.

Few know this, but Walt Disney went bankrupt. Fired from a newspaper in 1919 for lack of imagination and good ideas, Walt decided to open his first company, an animation and film studio, which went bankrupt in 1922. What's more, even after creating the most famous character in the world, Disney ended up losing his funding with the production of his first film (Snow White and the Seven Dwarves) and had to resort to a bank loan. After the film's release, money was never a problem for Walt Disney again. The inventor of Mickey Mouse won 32 Oscars and the Walt Disney Company, started in 1923, is to this day one of the most powerful in the market.

LET'S TALK!

Look at some examples of famous people's resilience:

STEPHEN HAWKING:

The most renowned theoretical physicist and cosmologist of his day did not let his serious physical condition affect the success of his career – quite the opposite! In addition to having three children, a grandson and countless awards received in recognition of his scientific studies, Hawking is a legend when it comes to physics and cosmology!

But for those who don't know, Stephen Hawking was diagnosed at the age of 21 with amyotrophic lateral sclerosis, a serious disease that gradually paralyzes all the muscles in the person's body.

More than 50 years after his diagnosis, Hawking had almost no control over his own body, but that never stopped him from continuing to work and attain extraordinary achievements – including participation in some television series and films!

Hawking had every reason to live isolated in a gloomy house on top of a mountain, ignoring everyone and everything, due to his physical condition. But the astrophysicist is a great example of resilience for having managed to overcome the adversities that arose throughout his life very well and to adapt fully.

Resilience is one of the most used words to describe Mandela. After five decades of struggle, Nelson Mandela (1918-2013) was elected the first Black president of South Africa, but before that, the leader fought against an intense and perverse regime of racial segregation and discrimination – apartheid. His strength and desire to help people who suffered from prejudice not only resonated on the African continent but became an example for the whole world! And even after 27 years imprisoned in a tiny cell, only a few meters long, and deprived of being able to see his family for almost three decades, Mandela showed no hatred or desire for revenge when he was finally released, but a great serenity that was transmitted through his speeches that crossed the world: "Nobody is born hating another person for the color of their skin, or their past, or their religion. People learn to hate, and if they can learn to hate, they can be taught to love, because love comes more naturally to the human heart than its opposite." A Nobel Peace Prize winner (in 1993), Mandela is one of the clearest examples of human resilience.

These people went through tragedies and were able to overcome adversity and deal with misfortunes.

NELSON MANDELA

Read the following story:

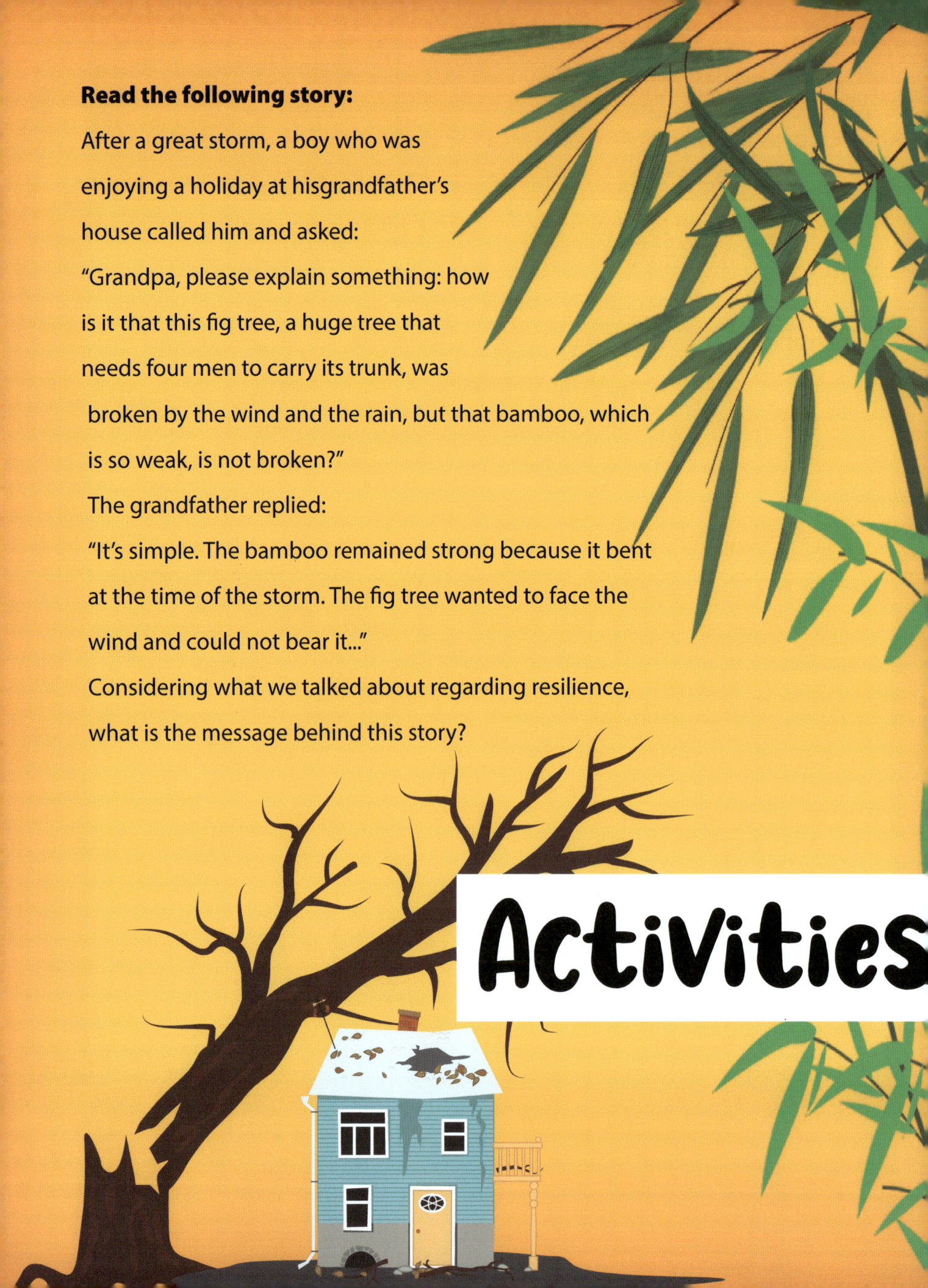

After a great storm, a boy who was enjoying a holiday at his grandfather's house called him and asked:

"Grandpa, please explain something: how is it that this fig tree, a huge tree that needs four men to carry its trunk, was broken by the wind and the rain, but that bamboo, which is so weak, is not broken?"

The grandfather replied:

"It's simple. The bamboo remained strong because it bent at the time of the storm. The fig tree wanted to face the wind and could not bear it..."

Considering what we talked about regarding resilience, what is the message behind this story?

Activities

Based on what you have learned so far about resilience, which of the figures below show resilience?

Have you ever had an experience of overcoming something that you had difficulty in learning? Write or draw below.

How did you face it? Write or draw below.

What have you learned from this situation? Write or draw below.

As we have seen, resilience is an effective way to deal with and to overcome problems. Considering that, search the internet for three cases in which someone had to overcome a difficult situation, different from the examples mentioned in class.
Then summarize each of the stories below.
You can explain to your parents or teacher or you can write the summary below.

1

2

3

WAYS TO TEACH RESILIENCE

STEP 1: Build a space where the child feels valued and recognized for his/her effort and dedication.

STEP 2: Bet on examples. Present stories of real or fictional characters who have overcome difficulties along the way.

STEP 3: Do not satisfy all wishes. Even if they take care of the child's well-being, parents need to encourage their child to solve some challenges alone in order to increase the child's self-confidence.

STEP 4: Avoid overprotecting your child, as if he/she is in a bubble. Protect your child from dangers, but allow him/her to make a mistake and start over.

STEP 5: Do not give ready-made answers. Instead of explaining all the "whys" directly, encourage your child to research and demonstrate that he/she is capable of discovering his/her own solutions.

STEP 6: Encourage perseverance. Learning sports or a musical instrument, for example, shows that you can only evolve with practice, dedication, discipline and overcoming your own limits.

STEP 7: Encourage children to set goals, such as a higher grade at school, a tidier room, more books read per year, being part of the school team, and so on.

STEP 8: Encourage empathy and positivity. Putting yourself in the other person's shoes and seeing the good side of situations helps you to face adversity.

It is crucial that your child realizes that it is normal to experience unpleasant or intense emotions and that these are fleeting. This should encourage children to face obstacles, teaching them how to use strategies that allow them to remain calm, as they will be able to process the situation more clearly and make thoughtful decisions.

Optimism and resilience go hand in hand. Help your child discover that all experiences have a positive or learning side. When difficult situations cannot be avoided, being resilient will be your child's best "protective shield."

Congratulations on completing this class and gaining more RESILIENCE.

Sending a hug to everyone!

Keep it up and we'll see you in the next episode.

Academic Team
KeyWords Education

Printed in Great Britain
by Amazon